GOD and ME in THREE

From yellow-dead man walking to child of God

Simon Flett

Onwards and Upwards Publications
11 Nightingale Crescent, West Horsley, Surrey KT24 6PD, UK
www.onwardsandupwards.org

First published 2011 in the UK by Simon Flett.
Second UK edition 2011.

ISBN: 978-1-907509-29-2

Cover design: Leah-Maarit

Printed in the UK

Author's Note

All enquiries concerning this book should be addressed by email to **simonflettox4@live.co.uk**

Profits from the sale of this book will go towards financing future YMCA projects in Europe for young people in recovery, ex-offenders or unemployed.

Acknowledgements

I have so many people and organisations I want to thank, so I am sorry if I miss anyone.

I want to thank the staff at Western Counselling Services where my journey began, especially the governor, Alan Davies, who believed in me and many other people.

To all the staff at Andrew House and at Clevedon YMCA, especially to Neil Wylie my mentor and Ian Eisentrager for believing in me and giving me the chance to coach boxing.

To the St. Mary's Youth Group staff, Jane Bird and Dr. Caroline Parfitt.

To the community of Clevedon for support and the young people for letting me work with you.

To all the friends I made along the way, past and present; you know who you are.

I want to say a big thank you from everyone in recovery to Big John who does so much for people.

To my mate, who has known me all my life, Tony Barratt, also known as Beefy, and his family who have supported me in my journey.

To a special lady, Jess Pattullo. I told you I would never forget what you have done for me.

I cannot forget the Donnington Estate in Oxford for some mad, mad times and to all of God's houses for even better times.

I want to say a big thank you to my editor and true friend Bernard Grimsey and to Margaret Spivey and Clive Harrison who have made this book possible.

And finally I have saved the best to last: my Mum, Dad, my sisters Samantha and Laurie and their children Antione, Marco, Ashley, Jordan and Andrea. You have seen me at my worst, and it was not a pretty sight. Thank you for sticking with me and letting me back into your lives. Words cannot describe the love I have for you.

And, oh yeah, to the ice cream man who used to give me an extra flake in my Mr Whippy!

Contents

About Me and Why I Wrote the Book

Well this is it.
This is how it's going down.
This is how we are going to do it.
First and foremost I just want to say,
"I love you, Jesus, my Saviour!"
I have a direct line to God
who has given me a life beyond my wildest dreams,
and that's what I want to share with you.

I want believers and non-believers,
I want people who are struggling, people with wealth, health
*   and happiness,*
I want people who are messed up, insecure, tooled up and
*   insane,*
I want people who are alcoholics, addicts of all sorts,
I want people who have tried every sort of self-help group
*   there is,*
and still got no reply.

I want people who wake up each morning
and still don't see the glory of the dawn calling,
to know what it's like to wake up each morning
with God as your personal alarm clock calling.

That's right, I want everyday people, like you and me to know what God has been doing in my life; and this is only the beginning. I have only found God's purpose for me in the last three years. Yes, that's right, I have only found my faith for about three years, and I just want people to know what a blessing it is.

In fact I want people to know that it is their right to know, and it is my duty as a servant of God to tell them, what it's like to walk with the Big Fella upstairs, how he has twisted and turned my life around, how he is shaping and moulding me to be the man he wants me to become. I want everyone to understand the impact he has had on my life in the last three years. That's right, I will say it again - *three years* - and it is only the beginning. Like hot porridge in the morning, God is stirring me up and making me glow to show he is calling me.

Blimey, I could go on and on about bigging up the Big Fella upstairs, but I hear him calling me.

In order for you to understand why this is such a big thing for me, I am going to have to tell you a bit about my past. Now I know what you are thinking – not that I do other people's thinking for them – you're thinking:

> *"Here we go with another sob story about how bad it was for*
> *him, and how he has done this crime and that crime.*
> *'Poor me. Poor me. Pour me another drink.'"*

I think you get what I am saying.

But it isn't going to be like that.
That's not progression. That's not moving forward.

We all know how to get messed up, insecure and insane.
We all know how to make a pig's ear of life.
It is what we humans are good at when we are left to our own devices and do our own thinking.
Well, this is where it all goes wrong for me.
I get all sorts of weird and wonderful and crazy thoughts going on, every morning, without fail – but

> *I hand it over to the power and care of God.*
> *I let him take it and deal with it so he can go on shaping*
> *and moulding me to the man he wants me to become.*
> *I need God to show me love and guidance at the start of*
> *every day.*

And what a glorious morning that is, with everything lifted off your shoulders and handed over to the care of God. You are stripped bare so every day is a new beginning, full of fresh, funky, loving ideas.

And that is the message I want to try and get across in this book. It's that I have found a new way of living that is fresh and clean - like the Colombian coffee bean - with fresh, funky, loving ideas. Now that cannot be a bad way of starting each morning, can it?

So let me get the dark, dull grey bit of my life over, so I can tell you how I came to know the glory of God.

And this is how I am going to do it.
Live and direct.
In your face.
Have some of this true grit.
I have not got time to mess about. So here goes.

Drugs – many.
Alcohol – smashed it.
Crime – all sorts.
Police – my fair share.
Courts – in and out.
Prison – been there, done it.
Hospitals – they had a big 'Welcome' mat outside the
A&E door with my name on it – but why would I care?

I have gone insane, gone yellow,
Had a wet brain and forgot my name,
I have pissed myself, shat myself and did not bother to
groom or wash my hair.
If you looked in my eyes you'd see the devil's glare.
I became criminally insane.
I mentally and physically hurt people.
I felt nothing - why should I care?

I hope you get the picture because I sure did, and believe me it was not the picture I was looking for. But this is the picture I want to share.

I want to share it with the suffering alcoholic and addict out there.

I want to share it with those who are in recovery.

I want to share it with the men, women and children who are banged up in prison because it was the insanity of their thinking that got them there.

May this book give you hope, faith and a belief that you can hang on in there.

I want to share it with everyday, ordinary people.

I want to share it with all of God's children out there.

That's right – that's you, that's me, that's every human being out there.

I have a direct line to God who has given me a life beyond my wildest dreams, and that is what I want to share with you. Jesus has been my Saviour.

So I will leave it at that. This is my book of hope. It is all true and comes from me to you. May you find what I have found, especially if you are a yellow-dead man walking. God is still working in my life and always will be.

The Every Morning Prayer I Say to Kick Start my Day

Every morning, without fail,
from the moment I open my eyes,
as soon as I hear God's alarm clock calling,
before I even think about or do anything else,
I give praise to the Big Fella upstairs.
I hand my life over to the care of God
each and every morning without fail.
I need God's help,
and I want him to fill me up with his Spirit,
and this is the prayer I say each and every day
to get my spiritual guidance that gets me through
a beautiful clean and serene day.
I say it and believe it with passion. I say it from the heart.
So when you read it, read it from the *heart*.
If and when *you* pray, say it with passion and conviction.
It's better than any two-bob drug,
or two-bob whore, better than a score.
Just close your eyes and feel God's love;
he wants to give it all to you.

READ THE PRAYER ON THE FOLLOWING PAGE.

So that's the prayer I say every morning
without fail - just like that. God's love is free, man.
It's FREE; come and get it!
It's the best fix you will ever have in your life.
Ask for it; then spread it thick like butter on crumpets!
You know what I'm saying?

Morning, Big Fella! How you doing? All good I hope.
What a beautiful day it is
and I just can't wait to get cracking on with it
and doing it with you.
I've got a lot on today so come and spend it with me
and help me out through the day.

And Jesus, come into my life;
come into my life, please, Jesus.
Fill me up with your Spirit;
fill my boots up with your Spirit.
Fill me up with your joy, your love, your happiness.

Your life, your belief, your career -
please, Jesus, come into my life and keep filling me up with
    all these things.
Keep filling me up with your knowledge, your wisdom,
your joy, your love, your happiness.

And as I go about my daily business,
help me to spread it to other people along the way,
to glorify your name, to glorify your kingdom,
to let people know what it is like
to walk with the Big Fella upstairs,
and whatever I do, to do it with a big grin on my face.

I just want to thank you for all the food and friendships,
love and guidance, time and money
you will be providing me with throughout the day.
I love you Jesus; let's have a brilliant day!
Up and at 'em brother! Amen.

A Place to Grow and Mature as a Person and in Faith

This is it – this is where it really all began for me.
This is where I started to grow as a person and in faith.
This was my next stage to independent living
after leaving rehab.
And WOW! What a little gem of a place!
In this little seaside town of Clevedon
there was this big bold house called
Andrew House, a Christian Care Home.
It is the next stage you move on to after leaving rehab
to ease you back into society and to get you used
to leading a clean and sober life.

As soon as I arrived at this house
I just knew that I was supposed to be there.
I just knew that God had sent me there for a reason.
It just felt right, so right,
even if it was in the middle of Somerset!
I mean, imagine sending a recovering alcoholic and addict
to the county home of cider making!
I mean it makes sense to me; that's the first place you would
think of, isn't it? Ha, ha!

Anyway, this was a speech I gave on my time in Andrew House
and what it and the staff meant to me:
(Like it says in the speech, it really is a special house
which is run by special people –
the staff and people of Clevedon.)

The Speech: Andrew House

Morning, everyone!

When my mates, Rob Johnson and Alan Goddard, asked me if I would like to say a few words about Andrew House and the work that goes on in there, I didn't have to think twice. I jumped at the chance, because I've got pure love for the place.

For those of you who don't know what Andrew House stands for, then let me tell you.

On paper its official description is a Dry House, the next stage for independent living in the community after leaving rehabilitation after drug and alcohol misuse, and to help you get settled in a community.

Now let me give you my interpretation of what it means to me.

It means a house of recovery, and a house of fellowship,
with its ups and downs like a merry-go-round.
A house of love.
A house where you can gain knowledge, wisdom and be given
opportunities to discover the meaning of life.
A house where you can grow and mature spiritually as a person
if you wish to do so.
I have seen it happen.
It's a house where a young or old man can walk in and be given
a new purpose in life. And that purpose is life. Live LIFE!
It's a house where you can really make your dreams come true.
It's God's house.
And with the loving encouragement and guidance from the
staff who work there, you can start putting all the pieces back
together to re-build a fruitful life.

You see, it's not just about putting down the drink and drugs –

it's about changing the way you are thinking,
it's about working on your issues,
it's about developing skills,
it's about twisting your life around and growing as a person

...and living with twelve other blokes who are also going through life-changing decisions, who feed and learn off each other.

Put this together with the tools that Andrew House has to offer:

patience, guidance, love and trust,
and if you put your energies into it
there is only one outcome –
a beautiful serene life.

And that's what Andrew House and God have given to me.

It really is a special house
which is supported and run by special people,
and that's the staff and community of Clevedon.

I have since moved on from Andrew House to independent living in Clevedon, where I am growing...

more and more in my faith and
more and more as a person,
and building up a fast and exciting career
with various projects on the go.

As I go about my daily business, I always pop into Andrew House, because I know the doors are always open, and I'm made to feel welcome any time of day or night. And no matter what's going on in my life - good or bad - I know I can offload to someone who will always give me the time of day.

Do you know what? It's my family home – it's family.

My First Testimony

WOW! This is the first testimony I ever did. My very first one. I chuckle to myself because I remember how nervous I was. I have done lots of crazy things in my life and I have been in a lot of off-key situations that make your body shake. I could chat breeze all day long when I was out in the madness buzzing my little nut off. But this was something else. I never had a feeling like this before. It was a fresh natural clean and sober feeling. I didn't have any drink or drugs inside me. And there I was about to go in front of a church congregation of about 180 people including the Bishop of Bath and Wells! That's right – the Bishop of Bath and Wells. I was going to tell them about my journey into faith and how Jesus came into my life. Like I said before, I have done some off-key things before this, but - WOW - this was something else!

I was nervous and so excited at the same time. I didn't know what I was thinking or feeling at the time. All I know is that it felt right; it just felt so right. I was buzzing off life. I was having fresh, funky, loving, clean and crisp feelings. There was love in the air, and I knew Jesus was there. I just knew.

Anyway, I will leave it there and hope you enjoy my first ever testimony on how I came to faith. I hope it gives you an insight into the person I once was, and how letting a power greater than myself into my life is helping to shape and mould me and restore my sanity. *And that person is God.*

Enjoy! I know the Bishop did! Ha, ha!

The Testimony

Hello there, everyone!

Cor blimey, it's like standing up in court again! Ha, ha! Anyway, where do I start?

When Russ phoned me up, out of the blue, and asked if I would like to say a few words about my journey into faith, I said, "Yeah, I'd love to, because I've never ever done it before."

He then said, "It's on the 13th June."

I paused for a minute and then said, "Wow, that's when my Mum and Dad's coming down. I can read it out to them as well."

It was like God had it all planned, just like he's got my life planned in his direction and in his time.

So let me tell you how I came to the glory of God. In order to do that I will have to tell you a bit about my past. Now I ain't got time to dribble on, so in a nutshell this is it:

Drugs – I've done them all.
Drunk till I couldn't drink no more – I was yellow.
Crime till I couldn't crime no more.
I've even robbed from inside my own front door.
Prison – done that.
Police cells – in and out.
Coppers always knocking at my Mum and Dad's front door.
Hospitals in and out after knocking at death's door.

I've done it all.

I really have done some mad and bizarre things.

I sold myself short and had no morals.

Now let's get down to business and talk about the glory of God and how it all began for me.

I went into rehab on May 1st 2007 in Weston-super-Mare, for drug and alcohol issues, where I did six months' rehabilitation. During this time I was allowed to go to church every Sunday if I wanted to.

I don't know what it was at the time,
whether it was the worship,
the people,
or because it was different,
but it was something – it just felt right.
I just felt I belonged there, and I got a buzz from it.
I didn't need no drink, drugs, women, money – nothing;
it was just there.

And in rehab you have to work on the issues surrounding your life, like the insanity of your behaviour, guilt, shame, resentments and so on. It's not all about just putting down the drink and drugs.

Anyway, I was working on these issues, but not easily. My counsellor told my Mum and Dad that it wasn't until the last three months of my treatment that I started to adjust to the programme; it was just around the time that I went up for my first prayer ministry at church and asked Jesus into my life.

I kept seeing people going up for prayer, so up I went and I told them my story and what I was finding hard to deal with. So we prayed on it and asked Jesus into my life. Then I went out of the church and I felt *whoooosh*!

I don't know; I just felt clean fresh, awake, light, empty -
no worries, no resentments, no guilt, no shame.
I just felt new. I had a new bounce in my step.
I was bouncing back to the rehab ... bounce ... bounce!
And I've not stopped bouncing since.

And that was it; now I did the rest of my time in rehab...

with God's direction.

And then...

Leaving rehab and going into Andrew House, a Christian Care Home, where I was able to mature and grow strong in faith through bible study -

that's God's direction.

Walking through the doors of the YMCA, a Young Man's Christian Association –

that's God's direction.

Responding to an invitation to be in a religious play as one of Jesus' disciples – Simon of all people! I didn't even know the scriptures –

that's God's humour and direction.

Meeting the producer, a retired minister, Rev Bernard Grimsey, who has become one of my best mates in Clevedon and with whom I have brilliant fellowship –

that's God's direction.

Taking charge of St Mary's Church Youth Group –

that's God's direction.

Doing some work in St Paul's Church and watching other people grow and helping them to find their faith –

that's God's direction.

Undertaking the Alpha Course –

that's God's direction.

Coming to this church and growing and maturing spiritually as a person –

that's God's direction.

You see, what I'm trying to say is, all this – and this is only a little bit of what God has done in my life - has happened in the last three years. And what you've got to remember is that during this time I have been battling addiction and the insanity of my old behaviour, which, believe me, was so off-key.

There is only one way that I have been able to do this and that's with the love and guidance of God.

Psalm 1 says:

They are like trees planted along the river bank
bearing fruit each season,
their leaves never wither
and they prosper in all they do.

My relationship with God is *my* relationship,
and he knows me inside out,
and he knows my heart is pure,
because he has changed it.
And he also knows that I'm only human
and I can be off-key and get it all wrong
just like the next man.

But as long as I keep putting all my energies in the right direction... and you know what direction that is, don't you?

God's direction!

I won't go wrong again.

And don't think for one minute that I would come to this church and not send out my love to my Mum and Dad who I have been truly blessed with. They have shown me love and kindness and provided me with nothing but the best all their hard-working lives, and much, much more. And through this journey they have supported me and believed in me in everything I do.

Mum and Dad, I love you. I've got pure love for you. You know I love you.

Thanks for listening to what I've had to share.
I love you Jesus, my mate, my Saviour, the man with my plan.
He might even have a white van!
One God, Amen.

Lyric from a Recovering Mind

This is a poem I wrote on my first birthday. My first whole year living a clean and sober life. I have just dug it out from my recovery folder. I had forgotten I did it. Cor blimey, it brought back some memories...

I remember sitting in the garden of my dry house on a hot May 1st with a big grin on my face and looking at all my tomatoes and lettuces that I was growing in the green house, and thinking to myself, "Wow, life is bliss! Live life! Love life! I've done a whole year clean and sober - *one whole year*! I can't believe it."

I remember sitting in the garden smelling clean fresh air - and me smelling fresh and clean. And my head was not pickled or in a daze; I just felt fresh and clean. Nothing to worry about. Nothing. Not a care in the world. So I just put pen to paper, and this is what I came up with. Hope you enjoy it.

Oh, yeah, throughout my journey of recovery and into faith I've kept a folder of all the bits and bobs I've done or achieved. It's good to reflect on what you are doing in life. And I remember thinking how special clean and sober memories are; they are the best memories, they are the memories I want. Live life! Live a beautiful, clean and serene life, and walk with the Lord.

Sit back and take it in.
This is where I begin.
BAM! Eyes wide open!
It's a new dawn; it's a new day.
Let's see what my recovery programme brings me today.

Lift my head off the pillow -
no sweating, no hecking, no kecking, no shaking -
that's always a good sign.
I think I will follow this recovery programme today.

Have a shit, shower and shave
And thank the Lord my head's not in a daze.
I think I will follow this recovery programme today.

I'm all fresh and clean.
My garms have just come out of the washing machine,
crisp and clean like the Colombian coffee bean,
speaking of which I'll have a mug of that;
it will kick start my day
to the recovery programme I will follow today.

To blossom in parts
and where my new life starts,
it's all about following the recovery programme today.

As I am thinking of what I should do for the rest of the
    day,
I hear this booming voice say,
"Kneel down and pray, and be true to yourself
and the rest will follow,
because you are following the recovery programme today
- just for today."

It's all about being true to yourself
and being true to the people
who will be true to you.
Don't let the bastards grind you down!

A Godly Tale 1

During the three years I have been walking with the Big Fella upstairs and becoming a Christian man, I have had what I call 'godly experiences'. They happen in all sorts of weird and wonderful ways. I pray on stuff and ask God for advice, love, support and guidance. I just chat to him and ask him to help me with stuff I am finding hard to deal with. It could be anything – big or small. I just chat to him and ask him to show me how to deal with something I am finding difficult.

One one particular occasion, I was finding it hard to go back to Oxford because it was there I did all my using, abusing, hurting and robbing, and made a right joker of myself. I had not been back in two years. I just packed my bags and went off to rehab in Weston-super-Mare - and that was that. But Oxford was always on my mind, because it was the place where I grew up. I had had good times there as well as the bad times, plus I had family and friends there. But I also knew I had people who despised me and who did not want me there.

I was always praying about this situation. I wondered if I was strong enough to go back and who would be after me if I did. Basically, I was too scared to go home, too scared of what people were still thinking of me. And if I did roll up in Oxford, would people think I was still that same insane person I was before I went away? Anyway, I kept praying about this situation, and this is how the Big Fella answered me.

I was asked if I would help out at a local charity shop in Clevedon. They wanted someone to go out on the vans one day a week to deliver and pick up stock around the Somerset area.

I had a bit of time on my hands, so I said, "Yeah, why not? When and where would you like me to start?"

Trisha, the manager of Cancer Research, said, "Be outside the shop at 8 a.m. A guy called Nigel will pick you up in the van, and you will go round Somerset collecting all the clothes."

So Friday morning came, and I made my way down to the charity shop in town and waited outside. Then this guy who I had never met before rolled up in this wagon, opened the door, and introduced himself as Nigel.

I said, "You all right, Nigel?"

He said, "Yeah, not bad - just a bit puzzled."

"Why's that?" I said.

Nigel replied, "For some reason we have to go to Oxford and do a delivery to a charity shop down there. I've done this job for years and I've never been asked to go to Oxford – never."

I looked at this bloke (and remember, I had never met this man before) and with a big grin on my face I said, "Nigel, we are going to Oxford for a reason."

I just knew.

So on the way down I told him my whole story - the journey of my life before I got into trouble, my journey into rehab and my journey into faith. I told him the whole lot. And I told him about my doubts about the journey home.

I told him I thought that something was going to happen in Oxford that day. I just knew that the Big Fella had something planned. At first I could tell that Nigel was looking at me and thinking, "I've got a fresh one here, still off his nut on drugs!"

But the more I was talking to him, the more he was listening. It was like I was preaching to him and he was listening and listening. By the time we got to Oxford it was like we had known each other for ages. He could have been a Christian brother.

Anyway, we roll up to Oxford, to a part I know well and where I used to do some of my using and drinking. So I was a bit on edge, plus my head was wondering what was going to happen. I just knew that something would happen.

So we pulled up at the back of the charity shop and started to unload the books we had to deliver. Six other blokes came out to help, so we formed a line from the van to the shop and started to pass the books along it. But there was this one guy who kept looking over at me, not in a bad way, but staring at me, So I gave him the eye-ball and thought to myself, "What's his problem?"

Anyway, once we had finished unloading the books, this bloke who had been looking at me comes over and says, "Don't I know you?"

I said, "No, mate, you don't know me."

I was thinking I might have robbed him or something.

"No, mate, you don't know me," I said again.

Then he said, "Yeah, I do. It's Fletty, i'nnit?" (my nickname in Oxford). "Didn't you go to Cheney School?"

I looked at him hard and I said, "Yeah, that's right. Who are you?"

He told me his name, and then I remembered and we got chatting. I could not believe it; I used to go to school with this fella twenty years ago, missing out on lessons to go and burn ganja with him at the top of the school fields. I could not believe it. I had not seen this guy for nearly twenty years.

So we carried on chatting, and he asked me what I was up to. I told him my story - everything. And he looked at me and said, "It's unbelievable. D'you know what? I'm in recovery for drug and alcohol misuse as well, and I work in this charity shop trying to sort my life out and put it back together again." He said, "This is unreal. I was having a bad day thinking what's it all about - life's boring - and you turn up and tell me your story. It's just unbelievable, and it's given me hope."

He then told me that the other five guys with him were on day release from prison. And they were trying to sort their lives out before they went back into society. So we all sat round in the back of the charity shop, and I told them my story and how I was doing my recovery and how I let God in to my life and how he was working in it.

Then I told them about never coming to Oxford until now and how I knew God had sent me to Oxford for a reason, to bump into these guys. They were blown away by how much a person could change. They thought it was impossible to find what I had found in such a short space of time. I said it was because I let God into my life. I know they went back to their cells with a word from God in their hearts.

And do you know what God did that day? He brought convicts and ex-cons together, people who were struggling and afraid to give each other hope and show that you can change. People change, circumstances change, life itself changes. Don't be afraid. That's what God did that day - he showed me people and things change. You have to change, so go and encourage others to change.

And we had a witness in Nigel who was just an ordinary bloke going about his daily business but blown away by what he saw. On the way back he just chatted and chatted on and on about what he had seen that day.

He said, "How did you know something was going to happen like that? How did you know?"

I told him, "I've been praying on a message from God, and when you pulled up and said we were going to Oxford, I just knew something was going to happen."

Nigel was not a Christian or a believer, but he said the 'God' word a few times on the way back.

Healthy Mind, Body Spirit and Soul

During my many years of being out there in the madness,
the only thing I was fuelling my body on
was drink, drugs and sausage rolls.
I absolutely battered my body inside and out.

During the last few years of my drinking and abusing,
I could not put solid food in my body.
I had to have a drink so I could swallow and digest it.
My sleep patterns were all over the place.
My teeth had dropped out.
I was seeing and hearing things.
I was walking around as yellow as Bart Simpson.
I was pissing and shitting blood.
The lining of my stomach had gone.
My ulcers had burst and my body was slowly shutting down.
I was half dead on a hospital bed, more than once.
That's where my drink and drugs took me.

But the body is the most amazing thing.
I have twisted and turned my body around
from yellow-dead man walking to child of God.
I know God wants my body pure so he can feed me his Spirit.
Healthy mind, body, spirit and soul feed off each other.

During the three years since I have put down the drink, drugs
and smokes – that's right I don't even smoke any more –
I have built my body back up.
I eat healthily and I do regular exercise.
In fact, I enjoy exercise;
it is an important part of my life recovery programme.

As you grow in faith,
as you become a maturing person,
as your vision expands,
it is important that your body grows with it

and becomes totally restored so that it all fits together.

I give God all the glory!
He is at the centre of all I do.
So I am not channelling all my energies into just one thing.
I make sure I spread them out evenly
so that I can prosper in everything I do.
In recovery it is important not to swap one addiction for another,
because it is easily done.
But if I focus on God, I know everything will be good.

So I would just like to share my fitness programme with you, and what you have got to remember is that three years ago I was a yellow frail figure of a man and my liver was about to explode.

I was battered and on my knees
and I would probably be asking you for "a special brew, please."

FITNESS PROGRAMME	
Gym and Swim	twice a week
Circuit Training	twice a week
Boxing	twice a week
Coaching Boxing	once a week

Find your own fitness programme and believe in yourself, and with God on your side there is only one outcome – fighting fit.

And that is what I have found in boxing. It has given me much more than fitness; it has given me a structure, discipline and a belief in myself and much, much more. I want to thank Ian Eisentrager for getting my fitness levels through the roof and for turning my body from water into ice. Believe me, if you want to get fit with a decent bunch of guys and you live in North Somerset area, then check this geezer out – Ian Eisentrager at Clevedon YMCA - and watch your body blossom and grow fit.

And I just want to leave you with this list of famous Christian sportsmen – Evander Holyfield; George Foreman; Raul; Frank Lampard; Ronaldo; Theo Wallcot; Kaka, World Player of the Year 2007, who openly wears a shirt saying "I belong to Jesus"; The Brazilian Football Squad, who when they won the World Cup in 2002 all sat in the middle of the pitch and prayed.

All these men give God the glory.
It speaks for itself –

IF YOU ARE GOING TO TRAIN, TRAIN WITH THE LORD.

Addressing the YMCA

This speech means so much to me, so it was important I got it right. It is similar to my first testimony, because that is how much it means to me, and I know that it was all part of God's plan and direction for me that I went to the YMCA.

I was approached by the South West Area Manager, Angela Hall, who asked if I would like to say a few words about my time at Clevedon YMCA at the National Convention being held in Bridgwater.

I said, "Yeah, no problem."

It was then that she told me that it would be in front of three to four hundred people, including Tessa Munt, M.P for Wells and the Bishop of Bath and Wells. That's right! This was going to be my second talk in front of the Bishop of Bath and Wells. I could not believe it - my mate the bishop.

I wanted to get this speech just right and I think I did, so I won't go into much detail about it because it is all there in the speech. I hope it gives you some idea of how important the YMCA was for my progression in life recovery and also how much I love the place and all the young people in it, because they have helped me grow as a person.

Oh yeah - just to let you know that the bishop came up to me afterwards and shook me by the hand and said, "That's my boy!" I told you he was my mate. Big up the bishop!

The Speech: YMCA

Afternoon, everyone! How you all doing?
Wow, there's a lot of you here, isn't there.
I've said this line before, but I'll say it again:
Cor blimey, it's like standing up in court again –
Only this time I'm telling the truth!

When Angela asked me if I would like to say a few words about what I do at the YMCA, I thought to myself, "No!" But I *will* say a few words about what the YMCA does for me.

(Readers will already have read about my past so I won't repeat it here, but as it was largely a new audience I had to tell them what I had been through.)

This is where my new life starts to blossom and flourish.
On the 1st November 2008 I walked through Clevedon YMCA's doors.
Now believe me, I've walked through many doors:

Court doors,
Police doors,
Prison cell doors,
Hospital detox doors,
and now Clevedon YMCA doors.

I discovered these doors were God's doors -
Doors of opportunity and structure.
I didn't want to go back out of these doors, and I haven't.

From day one they knew all about me and my past,
but they didn't flicker an eyelid.
They just wanted to give and give;
and that's what they did – gave and gave.

They gave me opportunities;
they gave me structure;
they gave me ambitions;
they gave me life and personal development skills;
they gave me happiness, hope and a career;
they gave me a life, a pure, clean and serene life;

and they are helping to shape and mould me
to the man that God wants me to become.

My life has taken a major turnaround.
First and foremost I became a Christian. I love you, Jesus!
Secondly, I have become a youth worker.

I lead a church youth group.
I do one-to-one sessions with young adults who face difficult
    challenges in life.
I work on drug and alcohol issues,
And check this –
I even work in a school helping young people!

And that's not all.

Terry, a close mate of mine who also works at the YMCA, and I
had the privilege of taking ten young people who were in recovery,
ex-offenders or just unemployed, to Bulgaria to help renovate an
orphanage. Would you believe - I'd never even been on a plane
before?

All this (and this is only a little bit of what's going on in my
life) has come from a small little YMCA building in the middle of
Clevedon and the love and guidance from all the staff who work
there.

You know who you are – Russ, Lorna, Jill, Ian, Terry, and my
mate Foster. But there is one man who I want to mention in
particular - someone I have been blessed with - and that is Neil
Wylie, whose presence in that place plays such a major part of
what goes on in there.

Neil,

I want to thank you for giving me a life beyond my wildest
  dreams.
I want to thank you for believing and trusting in me.
I want to thank you for putting up with all my off-key and
  crazy thoughts.
I want to thank you for being a friend.

God gave me the gift of friendship, and I'm glad he gave me
you.
And that's what you get when you walk through the YMCA's
doors.

Now who in their right mind would want to walk back out of
those doors?
I would recommend any young person to go and push those
YMCA doors and see their life begin and blossom.

And don't believe for one minute that I would stand up here
And not send out my love to my Mum and Dad who I have
been truly blessed with and who I am glad are here today.
Mum and Dad: I love you! I've got pure and clean love for you;
you know I love you.

Thanks to you all for listening to my share.
I love you Jesus, my mate, my saviour,
the man with my plan –
he might even have a white van.
One God. Amen.

A Godly Tale 2

As you have just read in my YMCA speech, I mentioned about a trip that a friend and I organised for the YMCA. We had to get ten people who were in recovery, ex-offenders or just unemployed, to take part in a mission to Bulgaria to help paint and renovate an orphanage.

During the run up to this journey we had to put on fundraising events to raise the money to buy the materials to use out there. That was a mission in itself, but we got there in the end and raised all the money we needed.

Once we were out there, we had to share out the different jobs to be done at the orphanage; so we split into two groups. Each group had a different project to do. My group had to strip down the outside wall, render it, and repaint it, and then paint a goal on it and put up a basketball hoop. Finally, we would add the Clevedon YMCA logo and our names.

We had two weeks to do this in. So in the first week we stripped down the wall and rendered it, and in the second we painted it pink and put the goal on it and fixed up the basketball hoop. That just left us with two days to decorate the wall with our names and logo and make it bright and colourful for the orphanage.

So from the second-to-last day, we got our paint and stencils that we had made and started to put our names and logo on the wall. But we just could not get the paint to stay on the wall, and when it did it just dripped making the wall look a right mess. It just dripped and dripped everywhere. So we had to repaint the wall pink and start again. This happened a few times, and the more it happened, the more the group were losing interest, and time was not on our side. At the end of the day we were still left with a pink wall with nothing on it except a basketball hoop. It had no colour, imagination or pictures for the orphans, so we all felt a bit deflated and annoyed with ourselves. We had finished everything else, but not this. And we had one day to go.

So we had our debriefing session, and I said to the group that the only way we were going to get our names and logo on it was if we found a graffiti artist. But there is no chance of finding one of them in the middle of a country in the middle of nowhere, so "let us leave it and come back tomorrow." We packed up our stuff, left the orphanage and went back to the hotel. We arranged to meet downstairs so as to go to the bar in the village to have a few drinks and chill out before dinner.

Now pay attention, because what happened next just blew my socks off to the moon. We all walked into this bar in the middle of the village, and there was this guy standing there graffiti-spraying the walls. I just stood there and went numb. I could not believe what I was seeing; neither could the group. In the middle of this village, in the middle of Bulgaria, in the middle of nowhere, there was this man with his hair in a pony tail spraying these walls - just standing there spraying them. The group could not believe what they were seeing. But I just knew that God had sent him. This was no coincidence. A graffiti artist in the middle of this village, where people still go around in a horse and carriage, in the middle of nowhere, in the middle of Bulgaria, there was this graffiti artist just standing there spraying walls with his cans. God sent him, I just knew.

So I turned to our interpreter and said, "You see that guy over there? God sent him to spray our walls, and you've got to go and tell him our story and that God has sent him to us."

She looked at me and bluntly said, "No, I do a lot for you and I listen to all your stupid ideas, but you're not going to get me to go over there and say that. No chance."

But I kept on at her and she finally gave in.

So I went with her to tell her what to say to this bloke. She tapped him on the shoulder, and as I started to tell her what to say, he looked at me and said it was O.K. because he could speak English! But not only that, he was a Christian as well. How about that? A graffiti artist in the middle of a village in the middle of nowhere who spoke English and was a Christian brother!

I told him my story and he was just blown away. He told me that he lived in the capital, Sofia, and that he had never been to the village before. He had been told to come and start this job - "God's job," he said with a grin on his face.

The next day he came to the orphanage and started to spray the wall with our names and logo. I just sat there with the heat blazing down on me, surrounded by little orphans running around watching this man with the ponytail hair spraying the wall. I just sat there with a smile on my face thinking, "God the graffiti artist."

Stealing: One of the Ten Commandments

St. Andrew's Church in Clevedon was running a Sunday morning series called "Just 10". It was a ten week course on the ten commandments, and I was asked if I would do a talk on stealing and what it meant to me during my alcohol and drug addiction.

We have all done bad things in our life, we have all sinned, some more than others, some worse than others. It does not matter whether it is a packet of cheese and onion Tesco value crisps that make your taste buds go numb and your lips fall to bits or an MP's tax fraud to finance his mistress. Theft is theft; you cannot put value on theft.

I am sorry for all the people I have stolen from, and that is why I have done this book - to let people know that we can change and encourage others to change.

The Talk

Morning, everyone!

So the theme is stealing, and I've been told I have five minutes to talk about it. So don't let me steal any more of your time! Let me tell you about what robbing, begging and stealing meant to me, because it was something I was rather good at.

I robbed, begged, stole till I could steal no more.
I've ripped people off in their thousands,
I've robbed them red and raw -
shops, companies, off licences, pubs, houses and much more.
I've even robbed off my own front door -
not once, not twice but much more.
If it was not nailed to the floor
I would have it off your front door.
I robbed, begged and stole and much, much more
to feed my drug and alcohol addiction
which was off-key and pretty hard core.
And believe me, this is the breakdown version.
I could go on and on; there's lots, lots more,
but why would I want to give the devil's work
all the glory galore?

You see, while I was doing all these insane crimes, there were things I didn't even realise I was stealing, and they are the most important things of all.

I was stealing...

people's dignity, people's trust, people's love,
people's kindness, people's honour, people's belief in society.
I could see the things I stole,
but I didn't see the things that, on the whole,
hurt people more
when you invade their private store.
But that's what stealing does -

it makes you blind to the law.

But today I can take responsibility for that
because I let someone come and steal something from me.
I let Jesus into my life
and he stole my heart, so I can go to eternity.
I am so glad I let Jesus into my life to strip me bare
to do the restoration that was needed there
and shape and mould me to the man he wants me to become.
I love letting Jesus work deep inside me.

You see, people and circumstances don't decide your future.
God does, so look to him.
If you don't surrender to Christ,
you surrender to chaos.

Everyone surrenders to something - if not to God then to
expectations of others, money, drink, drugs, women, robbing,
stealing –
the list is endless; I could go on and on.
So for me there is only one way I want to live
and that's with the love and guidance of God,
and I hand over my life to his care every morning
to let him steal and fix another piece of me.

So in some cases stealing can be good.
For example, the only thing I want to steal today
is your heart and put a bit of God's love in it.
In fact, I know I have stolen something from you today
Because you are still here listening to me.
I stole a bit of your heart, and I put God's love in it,
so I'm glad I stole something off you today.

So let God into your life, I pray,
and let him steal a piece of you each day

I love you, Jesus! Amen.

A Summary of my Three Years with God and Me

In the three years of putting down the drink and drugs and handing my life over to the care of God, I have achieved the following things:

- ✓ Quit drink
- ✓ Quit drugs
- ✓ Quit smoking
- ✓ Quit crime
- ✓ Built up my health and fitness from being half dead
- ✓ Learned boxing and help with coaching
- ✓ Got my own flat
- ✓ Went to college and got qualifications in youth work
- ✓ Became a youth worker at the YMCA
- ✓ Work in a school supporting young people
- ✓ Taken disadvantaged young people away for a week
- ✓ Organised and taken part in fundraising events
- ✓ Taken 10 young people who are in recovery, ex-offenders or unemployed to Bulgaria to renovate an orphanage
- ✓ Lead a church youth group
- ✓ Member of the YMCA Board
- ✓ Received baptism
- ✓ Took part in a play
- ✓ Built up new friendships
- ✓ Given talks to various groups in churches and prisons
- ✓ Learned to drive
- ✓ Got a third paid job as a Senior Support Worker with young adults. (Three years ago I did not have *one*.)
- ✓ Wrote this book to glorify what God has been doing in my life
- ✓ Other bits and bobs, but I will leave it at that.

That's not bad for someone who has come from yellow-dead man walking to a child of God! I love you, Jesus, and need you like cooked food and onion.

Final Thoughts and Feelings

I guess that's it. That is just some, and I mean *just some*, of what God has been doing in my life. He has opened so many other doors and opportunities for me that I could go on and on. But I will leave it at that.

I hope you have got some insight into the sort of person I once was and to the person that God wants me to become.

The reason I did this book was to say to people

who are trapped in their guilt and shame as a result of crime,
who are going through their journey of recovery from addiction,
who are going through life-changing decisions,
who are trying to find out what a clean sober life is like:

"Let Jesus into your heart and he will teach you.
The teaching of Jesus will show you what's true."

I just want to leave you with these quotes from Helmut Thielicke and Fyodor Dostoevsky. I think they are a good way to end this book of hope from me to you.

Jesus gained the power to love harlots, bullies, and ruffians... he was able to do this only because he saw through the filth and crust of degeneration, because his eye caught the divine original which is hidden in every way in every man!... First and foremost he gives us new eyes ... When Jesus loved a guilt-laden person and helped him, he saw in him an erring child of God. He saw in him a human being whom his Father loved and grieved over because he was going wrong. He saw him as God originally designed and meant him to be, and therefore he saw through the surface layer of grime and dirt to the real man underneath. Jesus did not identify the person with his sin, but rather saw in this sin something alien, something that really did not belong to him, something that merely chained and mastered him and from which he would free him and bring him back to his real self. Jesus was able to love men, because he loved them right through the layer of mud.

Helmut Thielicke

To love a person means to see him as God intended him to be.

Fyodor Dostoevsky

The Prayer I Say to End my Day

Every evening of every night I give thanks to the Big Fella upstairs. Obviously, every day is something different, but I always start it off and end it like this.

Dear God, thank you for another day.
Thanks for a smoke-free day, clean and sober.
I just want to thank you for a beautiful and serene day.
I want to thank you for all the opportunities and people
you put into my life.
I want to thank you for all the love, support and guidance
you have shown me.

Will you send my love to all the people
who are struggling out there in the world?
May they find you.
Will you send my love to the people
who have not found the rooms yet,
to the people who have not found recovery,
who have not found the Church?
May they find what I have found,
because it is a blessing and I have been truly blessed.

Will you send my love to my Mum and Dad,
my sisters and their children,
Antione, Marco, Ashley, Jordan and Andrea?
Will you send my love to all my friends, past and present,
to the community and youth of Clevedon?
I just want to thank you for all the food and money you
have provided me with today.

I love you, Jesus. Amen.

From the Publisher

Titles in the **True Stories** series:

These books and more can be ordered from the publisher's web site:

www.onwardsandupwards.org